Usborne Workbooks

Times Tables

This book belongs to

....

There are answers on page 27, and notes for grown-ups at the back of the book.

Here are some of the jungle animals you'll meet in this book.
They are learning their times tables.

You can use a pen or pencil to help the animals with the 3, 4, 6 and 8 times tables.
Draw over the dotted lines and write the numbers in the boxes.

Usborne Workbooks

Times Tables

Illustrated by Marta Cabrol

Written by Holly Bathie
Designed by Maddison Warnes

Cheeky

Lem

Froggy

At the end of the book there are blank pages for more times tables practice.

Beaky

Edited by Jessica Greenwell
and Kristie Pickersgill
Series Editor: Felicity Brooks

Groups of 3

Lily pads grow in groups of 3 on the river. Can you trace the lily pads and finish Froggy's calculation for her?

Froggy

 X
group of lily pads **=** lily pads altogether

Count in 3s to complete the rest of Froggy's calculations. You could draw more groups of 3 lily pads in the river each time to help you.

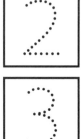 X  lily pads **=** lily pads altogether

 X lily pads **=** lily pads altogether

 X lily pads **=** lily pads altogether

 X lily pads **=** lily pads altogether

Crock

6	×	3	lily pads	=		lily pads altogether
7	×	3	lily pads	=		lily pads altogether
8	×	3	lily pads	=		lily pads altogether
9	×	3	lily pads	=		lily pads altogether

Write the next calculation yourself.

| | × | | lily pads | = | | lily pads altogether |

6 times

These 6 leopard cubs need some spots. Draw 1 spot on each leopard and then complete the calculation below.

$$6 \times 1 \text{ spot} = \square \text{ spots altogether}$$

Help Cheeky complete these calculations. For each one, you could draw 1 more spot on each leopard to help you.

$$6 \times 2 \text{ spots} = \square \text{ spots altogether}$$

$$6 \times 3 \text{ spots} = \square \text{ spots altogether}$$

$$6 \times 4 \text{ spots} = \square \text{ spots altogether}$$

$$6 \times 5 \text{ spots} = \square \text{ spots altogether}$$

Cheeky

| 6 | X | 6 | spots | = | | spots altogether |

| 6 | X | 7 | spots | = | | spots altogether |

| 6 | X | 8 | spots | = | | spots altogether |

| 6 | X | 9 | spots | = | | spots altogether |

Write the next calculation yourself.

| | X | | spots | = | | spots altogether |

8

The 3 times table

Here is the 3 times table. Trace the numbers and write the answers for Cheeky and her friends.

$1 \times 3 = 3$

$2 \times 3 = 6$

$3 \times 3 = $

$4 \times 3 = $

$5 \times 3 = $

$6 \times 3 = $

$7 \times 3 = $

$8 \times 3 = $

$9 \times 3 = $

$10 \times 3 = $

The numbers in the blue boxes are in the 3 times table.

3 6 9 12 15 18 21 24 27 30

The 6 times table

$1 \times 6 = 6$

$2 \times 6 = 12$

$3 \times 6 = $

$4 \times 6 = $

$5 \times 6 = $

$6 \times 6 = $

$7 \times 6 = $

$8 \times 6 = $

$9 \times 6 = $

$10 \times 6 = $

Help us finish the 6 times table.

Now draw a circle around the numbers in the 3 times table that are also in the 6 times table.

33 36 39 42 45 48 51 54 57 60

Patterns of 3 and 6

Tig has circled the first few numbers in the 3 times table on this number grid. Circle the rest for him.

Tig

> I've counted 3 three times to get to 9. 3 lots of 3 is 9.

1	2	③	4	5	⑥	7	8	⑨	10
11	12	13	14	15	16	17	18	19	20
21	22	23	24	25	26	27	28	29	30
31	32	33	34	35	36	37	38	39	40
41	42	43	44	45	46	47	48	49	50
51	52	53	54	55	56	57	58	59	60

Lep

Now draw a triangle around all the numbers in the 6 times table.

The numbers with both a circle and a triangle around them are in both the 3 and 6 times tables.

Now help Baz and Ant complete these calculations from the 3 and 6 times tables. You could use the number grid to help you.

9 × 3 =

7 × 3 =

7 × 6 =

3 × 3 =

6 × 6 =

9 × 6 =

8 × 6 =

Baz

I've seen some of these calculations before.

Ant

Multiplying with 3 and 6

Can you help the animals with this matching
game? Draw a loopy line to match each
question to its answer.

6 x 9

30

30

3 x 10

Where's my
matching card?

54

5 x 6

3   6   9   12   15   18   21   24   27   30

Groups of 4

The animals are collecting oranges, 4 at a time. Trace the oranges Tan-tan has found and complete her calculation.

Tan-tan

1 × 4 = ☐

Help Tig complete these calculations. For each one you could draw another group of 4 oranges in the trees to help you.

2 × 4 = ☐

3 × 4 = ☐

4 × 4 = ☐

5 × 4 = ☐

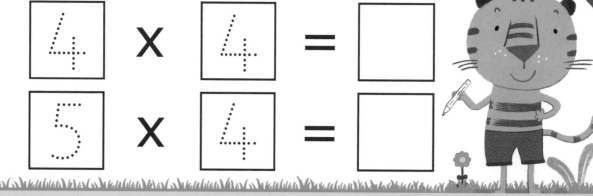

4   8   12   16   20

Write the next calculation yourself.

8 times

These 8 tiger cubs need some stripes. Draw 1 stripe on each tiger and then complete the calculation below.

$$8 \times 1 = \boxed{}$$

Help Baz complete these calculations. For each one, you could draw 1 more stripe on every tiger.

These numbers are double the ones in the **4** times table.

$$8 \times 2 = \boxed{}$$
$$8 \times 3 = \boxed{}$$
$$8 \times 4 = \boxed{}$$
$$8 \times 5 = \boxed{}$$

8   16   24   32   40

8 X 6 = ☐

8 X 7 = ☐

8 X 8 = ☐

8 X 9 = ☐

What a lovely sunset!

Write the next calculation yourself.

☐ X ☐ = ☐

48   56   64   72   80

The 4 times table

Here is the 4 times table.
Trace the numbers and fill in
the empty boxes for the animals.

The numbers in the blue boxes are in the 4 times table.

1 × 4 = ☐

2 × ☐ = ☐

3 × ☐ = ☐

4 × ☐ = ☐

5 × ☐ = ☐

6 × ☐ = ☐

7 × ☐ = ☐

8 × ☐ = ☐

9 × ☐ = ☐

10 × ☐ = ☐

4   8   12   16   20   24   28   32   36   40

The 8 times table

1 × 8 =

2 × =

3 × =

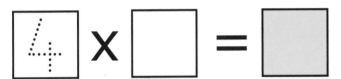

4 × =

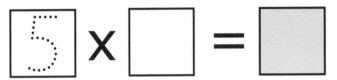

5 × =

6 × =

7 × =

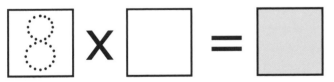

8 × =

9 × =

10 × =

Help us finish the 8 times table.

Now draw a circle around the numbers in the 4 times table that are also in the 8 times table.

44   48   52   56   60   64   68   72   76   80

Patterns of 4 and 8

Crock has circled the first few numbers in the 4 times table on this number grid. Circle the rest for him.

I've counted 4 three times to get to 12 3 lots of 4 is 12.

1	2	3	④	5	6	7	⑧	9	10
11	⑫	13	14	15	16	17	18	19	20
21	22	23	24	25	26	27	28	29	30
31	32	33	34	35	36	37	38	39	40
41	42	43	44	45	46	47	48	49	50
51	52	53	54	55	56	57	58	59	60
61	62	63	64	65	66	67	68	69	70
71	72	73	74	75	76	77	78	79	80

Now draw a triangle around all the numbers in the 8 times table.

Eight yummy ants!

Now help Lem complete these calculations from the 4 and 8 times tables. You could use the number grid to help you.

$4 \times 9 = \boxed{}$

$4 \times 7 = \boxed{}$

$8 \times 2 = \boxed{}$

$4 \times 4 = \boxed{}$

$8 \times 8 = \boxed{}$

$7 \times 8 = \boxed{}$

$8 \times 9 = \boxed{}$

Multiplying with 4 and 8

Can you help the animals with this matching game?
Draw a loopy line to match each question to its correct answer.

4 8 12 16 20 24 28 32 36 40

8 X 2

24

16

Can you see my matching card?

20

4 X 5

6 X 4

10 X 4

24

40

3 X 8

44 48 52 56 60 64 68 72 76 80

Times tables quiz

Find out how much you can remember about the 3, 4, 6 and 8 times tables by doing this quiz. Answers on page 26.

A. The animals are writing calculations for numbers that are in both the 3 and the 6 times tables. Complete their calculations.

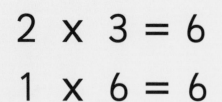

2 x 3 = 6

1 x 6 = 6

☐ X 3 = 12

☐ X 6 = 12

☐ X 3 = 18

☐ X 6 = 18

☐ X 3 = 24

☐ X 6 = 24

☐ X 3 = 30

☐ X 6 = 30

B. The animals are writing calculations for numbers that are in both the 4 and the 8 times tables. Complete their calculations.

2 x 4 = 8

1 x 8 = 8

☐ X 4 = 16

☐ X 8 = 16

☐ X 4 = 24

☐ X 8 = 24

☐ X 4 = 32

☐ X 8 = 32

☐ X 4 = 40

☐ X 8 = 40

C. Can you spot a number that is in the 3, 6, 4 and 8 times tables? Write it in this box:

D. Complete these 6 and 8 times tables calculations for Baz and Froggy.

6 x 6 = ☐

8 x 8 = ☐

8 x 6 = ☐

9 x 6 = ☐

7 x 8 = ☐

10 x 6 = ☐

9 x 8 = ☐

7 x 6 = ☐

10 x 8 = ☐

6 x 8 = ☐

E. Can you spot a number that is in both the 6 and 8 times tables? Write it in this box: ☐

Quiz answers

A.	B.	C.	D.		E.
4 x 3 = 12	4 x 4 = 16	24	6 x 6 = 36	10 x 6 = 60	48
2 x 6 = 12	2 x 8 = 16		8 x 8 = 64	9 x 8 = 72	
6 x 3 = 18	6 x 4 = 24		8 x 6 = 48	7 x 6 = 42	
3 x 6 = 18	3 x 8 = 24		9 x 6 = 54	10 x 8 = 80	
8 x 3 = 24	8 x 4 = 32		7 x 8 = 56	6 x 8 = 48	
4 x 6 = 24	4 x 8 = 32				
10 x 3 = 30	10 x 4 = 40				
5 x 6 = 30	5 x 8 = 40				

Score 1 point for each correct answer and write your score in this box: 28

Answers

pages 4-5

1 x 3 = 3	6 x 3 = 18
2 x 3 = 6	7 x 3 = 21
3 x 3 = 9	8 x 3 = 24
4 x 3 = 12	9 x 3 = 27
5 x 3 = 15	10 x 3 = 30

pages 6-7

6 x 1 = 6	6 x 6 = 36
6 x 2 = 12	6 x 7 = 42
6 x 3 = 18	6 x 8 = 48
6 x 4 = 24	6 x 9 = 54
6 x 5 = 30	6 x 10 = 60

pages 8-9

See answers to pages 4-5.

1 x 6 = 6	6 x 6 = 36
2 x 6 = 12	7 x 6 = 42
3 x 6 = 18	8 x 6 = 48
4 x 6 = 24	9 x 6 = 54
5 x 6 = 30	10 x 6 = 60

page 10

page 11

9 x 3 = 27	3 x 3 = 9
7 x 3 = 21	6 x 6 = 36
7 x 6 = 42	9 x 6 = 54
	8 x 6 = 48

pages 12-13

3 x 10 = 30	6 x 2 = 12
5 x 6 = 30	3 x 5 = 15
6 x 9 = 54	3 x 8 = 24
9 x 3 = 27	10 x 6 = 60

pages 14-15

1 x 4 = 4	6 x 4 = 24
2 x 4 = 8	7 x 4 = 28
3 x 4 = 12	8 x 4 = 32
4 x 4 = 16	9 x 4 = 36
5 x 4 = 20	10 x 4 = 40

pages 16-17

8 x 1 = 8	8 x 6 = 48
8 x 2 = 16	8 x 7 = 56
8 x 3 = 24	8 x 8 = 64
8 x 4 = 32	8 x 9 = 72
8 x 5 = 40	8 x 10 = 80

pages 18-19

See answers to pages 14-15.

1 x 8 = 8	6 x 8 = 48
2 x 8 = 16	7 x 8 = 56
3 x 8 = 24	8 x 8 = 64
4 x 8 = 32	9 x 8 = 72
5 x 8 = 40	10 x 8 = 80

page 20

page 21

4 x 9 = 36	4 x 4 = 16
4 x 7 = 28	8 x 8 = 64
8 x 2 = 16	7 x 8 = 56
	8 x 9 = 72

pages 22-23

8 x 10 = 80	4 x 5 = 20
4 x 3 = 12	6 x 4 = 24
8 x 4 = 32	3 x 8 = 24
8 x 2 = 16	10 x 4 = 40

Notes for grown-ups

Groups of 3 (pages 4–5)

This helps children to count in 3s and to link this to multiplying. You could encourage them to count up to 30 in 3s.

6 times (pages 6–7)

This helps children understand how the word 'times' links with multiplying. For the calculations 6 x 2, 6 x 3 and 6 x 5 you could encourage them to count the spots in 2s, 3s and 5s respectively to reach the right answer.

The 3 times table/The 6 times table (pages 8–9)

Children may notice that the numbers in the 6 times table are double the numbers in the 3 times table. This link may help children become more confident with remembering both tables.

Patterns of 3 and 6 (pages 10–11)

Multiples of 6 end in 6, 2, 8, 4 or 0. This repeating pattern helps children to predict further multiples of 6 without counting. (Multiples of 3 end in 3, 6, 9, 2, 5, 8, 1, 4, 7, 0. This pattern then also repeats.)

Multiplying with 3 and 6 (pages 12–13)

Children may realize that they can use times tables that they already know, for example the 2, 5 and 10 times tables, to help them answer some of these questions.

Groups of 4 (pages 14–15)

This helps children to count in 4s and link this to multiplying. You could encourage them to count up to 40 in 4s.

8 times (pages 16–17)

For the calculations 8 x 2, 8 x 3, 8 x 4, 8 x 5 and 8 x 6 you could encourage children to count the stripes in 2s, 3s, 4s, 5s and 6s respectively to reach the right answer.

The 4 times table/The 8 times table (pages 18–19)

Children may notice that the numbers in the 8 times table are double the numbers in the 4 times table. This link may help children become more confident with remembering both tables.

Patterns of 4 and 8 (pages 20–21)

Multiples of 8 end in 8, 6, 4, 2 or 0. This repeating pattern could help children to predict further multiples of 8 without counting. (Multiples of 4 end in 4, 8, 2, 6, 0. This pattern then also repeats.)

Multiplying with 4 and 8 (pages 22–23)

Children may realize that they can use times tables that they already know, for example the 2, 5 and 10, 3 and 6 times tables, to help them answer some of these questions.